Not Today

Lulu, Inc
860 Aviation Parkway
Suite 300
Morrisville, NC 27560

This is a work of fiction. Everything written herein is complete opinion of the author. Names, characters, places and incidents are products of the author's imagination or are used fictitiously.

Not Today

ISBN: 978-0-6151-5560-9

Printed in the United States of America

Cover illustration by Minimah Billings

10 9 8 7 6 5 4 3 2 1

Dedication

This is devoted to my dearest friends; Xavier F. Blackwell and Kenya R. Giles. Xavier, you taught me how to get down to the heart of the matter. When I didn't believe in myself you did. You pushed me and made me stay the course. It's astounding how you know me better than I know myself. We've shared some hilarious moments; you are my best friend. We've had our good days and our dire days and yet we've always persevered on. They simply don't understand us. Oh, well. You are a kind person and you have a wonderful heart. Continue to reach for the stars; for it's not that far. I incontrovertibly do love you. Kenya, you are the best sister one could *ever* have. I could have never dreamed to know someone who could care for me as the way you do. You've seen me at my best and you've seen me at my worst. In spite of it all, you continuously love me. Remember when mommy said that 'love is a misunderstanding between two fools'? Well, I guess I'm a spectacular fool because I will love you even pass the world's end. Will the world ever end? Ha! You are a wonderful sister and a superb mother but best of all, you are a fantastic friend. One can not select his family but one may choose his friends. I'm so glad that we were put together from the start but if I had to choose a friend I definitely would choose you. Thank you for blessing me with magnificent godchildren whom are my two beautiful nieces; Chanel and Tiffany. There are none better than these.

I could have never lived comfortably without those that are closest to my heart; my dear family. To my biological mother; Linda Billings, I thank you for giving me life and loving me unconditionally. To my foster mother; Martha Mickens, my gratitude for sharing your affectionate compassion with me in spite of the world's unyielding standards. You both have loved me beyond measure. You have taught me so much. I have been groomed to be a lady. May God rest your souls. To the rest of my beloved family, may you live on; Lillie Mae Billings, Kenya Giles, Kelly Williams, Marcus Williams, James Giles, Lucinda Porter, Jerome Billings, Emmanuel Billings, Chanel Robinson, Willie Mae Billings, Hope Hubbard, Tiffany Giles, Rev. and Mrs. Robert L. Cunningham, Johnny Billings, Mary Cunningham and Kamalah Brown. To my extended family which are my most cherished friends; Xavier Blackwell, Titus Robinson, Erecha Laney, Steven Stotts, Jr., Jennifer McDaniels, Jacquesh Cotto, Pastor Stephen D. Banks, Shaunte Blanchard, Onekia Grier, Felicia Foster, Joseph Graves, Courtney Williams, Tennille Dixon, Norman Belton, Ashlee Reynolds and Brandon Roberts. My life wouldn't make any sense without you. You are hidden treasures. I wish the world knew your hearts as I do. Whether you are one mile down the road or 15,000 miles across the vast deep sea; if I spoke to you last night or last year; I won't hesitate at all, at whatever time you call. We've been through the storms at times and on times have visited plains of glory. You can do anything. Go for the gold and don't stop.

I want to thank some people who are very special to me; Jill Telford. You help me make sense of what I write and point me the right way. I appreciate all of your help. You are a writer after my own heart and I wish you much success. Jayvonna Glaze, you understand exactly what I am saying and I recognize and value your gentle spirit. You are almost more excited about my writing than I am. I've met various people in my travels and I wish to thank you for your kindness, concern and cordiality. You know who you are.

I am not sure of how anyone could be a friend of mine for I am so stubborn at times. Heaven only knows. Ha! However, I must laugh aloud for I am undoubtedly changing…

Then, there are those who don't fancy the idea of me; well, I'm not quite certain of what to say to you, I am just me. If you don't like me then that is your problem not mine. Thank you for disliking me and doubting me; I have become so tenacious because of your distain for my being. Determined, yes, that's me.

Introduction

There are chronicles printed here in diverse ways of expressions. These chronicles are simply imperfections that I was bold enough to put on view. They consist of dozens of poems, several short stories, axioms and even a song. I hope that this work inspires you. If I can help you even in the smallest measure, make your day a little better or a little brighter than I have done my job. Sit back and relax and enjoy yourself. There will be times when you will want to laugh and then there'll be times when you will want to cry. I write a lot about love found, love lost, courage, trust, friendship, and the future. Some writings are extensive and several reasonably short in length. This endeavor is exceedingly delicate to me. There is so much that lies in my heart. If only I could get it all out onto paper…

While we often times wish to help ourselves accomplish set goals we must help others progress at the same time. Life is a circle of resources and if we don't help someone else than we are a waste of wealth. Helping is what I do best. I have a listening ear and an open heart. Everyone deserves a chance to succeed. It is not hard to succeed but it is very hard to fail. To fail means that you didn't even try. If you fall you can get back up and walk. Fall again then crawl. In the long haul you'll get to your destination unless you fall below your *own* expectation.

Ignorance is not a blissful state so I take the time to learn. Wisdom comes from the understanding of a past experience; so I reflect on what has happened. Every choice I have made in my life has led me to this point. Right now I am a full-time college student and it gives me great joy. At Cheyney University we are trying to create an honorable legacy for those to come.

As we need oxygen to breathe we need books to read. We can garner all the knowledge we possibly can from these compilations of writings (books). I worked in a library before and I could hardly breathe. I wondered if anyone realized how beautiful of a place it is. All those books; there are thousands and thousands of books waiting on us. There are books of inspiration, self-help, assistance, health and wellness, fitness and beauty, scholarly journals, essays, poems, short stories, children's stories, bibliographies and songs. Words are our own personal music; it's utterly beautiful. Give your life a song.

There are so many people in need and being able to help just one person smile because I reached out and helped them is such a great triumph for me. It's somewhat of an individual goal. I have so much to share with you; world and I highly enjoy writing for you. This is just the beginning.

Life has many challenges and we as a whole must face them. Life isn't easy but it sure is accomplishable. The mission is worth the fight you give it.

Under a weeping willow tree is where you'll find me…

Table of Contents

Chapter Two: Inspiration

The First Hiatus:

The Second Hiatus:

Not Today

Chapter One: Love

The First Hiatus

Invincible

The best I've ever *had* known
No one makes me mad
Distance can't separate us
The two of us are now one
One
Invincibly

Created in the heavens
Cool wind blown over my face
My eyes are closed wide shut
Shang *hi* noon
With a cool day

Sitting in one attitude
Watching birds fly
Reading
Singing
Ivory linen
Silken satin
Blue shoes
Roses dampened
Mix matched carpets
Gold mats
Purple hats
Velvet socks
Red sacks
Green beans
Oven mitts
Juicy juice sips

The super small smiled grin
The dimples on your cute chin

Things I think of
Sparkling water
Flowing over
Silver medallions
Kicking dust
Making crust
Apple pie
Or strudel
Drawing
Or doodle
Hot grits
How about noodles?
Warm soap

How will I cope?
I almost lost hope

Stop thinking of me
Even quit staring
I hear what you're saying
Every single day
Will it be that way?
6:28 PM 12/26/06

Intoxication: Our Story

It's the flight of the Phoenix
Only between us
Soaring high
After the take off
We flew so far
So fast

Where are we?
Are you there?
I can see you
We are so high

Oh, my
My dear
Loving you
Intoxicating
Your bright eyes
Staring at me
You can do so much
Because of me
All the colors I showed

Listen to my heart
It's calling out for you
My love
Whispering
Personal thoughts
Only things that
Together we've shared
Things no others would dare

Rebuttal

My life has been completely changed

Your eyes pierce directly through *mi* soul
Your mind looks right into my heart
And I become lost without you
What can I do without you?

Right now I am breathless
Continuously, I try to shake you
Yet you refute me
Your refusal to allow me to leave, condescends all forces of nature
Time measures our inconsistencies

Why do you give so little and take so much?

Validity settles close to the surface of my heart to be beat out by your biased lies
Reduction in my time spent with you is occurring
Unbeknownst to myself I am running away from your tainted love
3:18 PM 4/09/07

A Force To Be Reckoned With

Together we are unstoppable
A power couple we are

Come close to me

Building houses
Complexes
Chasing dreams
Swimming across streams
Fields of barley and wheat
Coming together we meet

Weeping willow trees
Sitting under them
We
Plan our futures
Business trips
Travel arrangements
Group plans
Wedding bells

Oh, my
"Wow"
There is magic here
Matrimony
Marital bliss

Sweet succulent kisses
From your miss
She is me
Melting in your arms

His and hers laptops
First class airplane seating
Eating right even in flight
Being active

The first of spring to spend with you
Not having to call to say "I simply love you"
Because I'm sitting right next to you
1:01 AM 12/27/06

Not Without You

Shoulda, coulda, woulda, but didn't
You should have loved me
You could have loved me
You would have loved me *but*
You didn't

You didn't love me
You never gave it a try
Something went horribly wrong

I didn't come here to tell you that I can't live without you
I surely can
I just don't want to
2:52 PM 4/09/07

Strong Lies

Some people are great liars
You sure are one of those I know
You stare right into my eyes and tell me things untrue
Why do you wish to continue to make me blue?

Oh how I trusted in you
There are millions of things I trusted in you

I gave up good and plenty
And turned *my* world into *our* world
I wonder why you did this to me

Ah
I know
I believed in you more than I believed in me
Never
No more
I'm an idiot
Pure

You made me so many promises
Promises that were empty
You gave me money you did
When I was in need
But I sure enough don't need you anymore

I did what you asked me to
You were so powerful with your lies that I gave days
Hours
Months of my time
I even went and got braces
You think that you are slick

My name is not Cassandra
And I repeat
I am not Cassandra
Its time to grow up

You've never took care of yourself
I can hear the dryer shaking the floor
It almost scares me
Not more than the way I trusted in you

What a liar
Pleasantly insane
Distained memories
It was you and I all the way
We behaved as modern day Bonnie and Clyde
In you I trusted and believed whatever you said

You
Liar
Lies
11:08 PM 5/15/07

The Getaway

I'm calling out for help
There's this man
He's in my life
He's wonderful but far from perfect
He makes fun of me

We both sing off key
We fight horribly but it doesn't break us up
We turn right around and make up
We often go to Infamous Wave's; it's a place he craves

Did I mention that we are the epitome of stubborn?
Only a few things are different between us
The rest is occult similarity
When he's around I refuse to sleep because I snore
He gets in a million minutes of rest plus more

And guess what?
He snores profusely
I refuse to close my eyes near him for he may find out that I'm imperfect
I tried to push him away but he won't budge
It's not that I don't love him
For I highly do
I can't see my life with him not in it

There's just one small problem; he wants to marry me
1:18 AM 5/27/07

Non-credible Love

Love has taken over me
Broken me down to simple green tea
Love has made me strong
It also has made me weak
So oft times I do not wish to speak

I've been blind
I've once had my sight
It made me cry
It has made me want to fight
I never wanted to lie

Yes, I wanted to die
It can't make me want you
But it sure has tried
Love won't let you fail
You can't beat it one bit

Love has made me rich
Love has made me poor
Love I never want anymore
It keeps taking over me
Especially when you are around
Why don't you just go away?

You *didn't* want me anyway
Please, don't stay
Run like you did before
Have me never more
Don't love me anymore
I don't want you to

I don't need you
You need you

I had a hope
You've stolen it
Give me my soul back
If you didn't intend to keep me
You should have gone your way

Now you're trying to stay
If you stay
Then stay
Be loyal
Be true
So to me
As I do to you
Give of yourself

Faithfully
9:17 PM 1/02/07

Tired

I'm saying goodbye, boy
I'm saying goodbye (chorus)
I'm tired of your lies, boy
I'm tired of your lies (chorus)
I'm leaving tonight 'ight
I know this is right (chorus)
You know that it's right (all)
Hush. Hush. Now, hush.

It's too late
It's too late (chorus)
For what you're about to say
You should've loved me when you had the chance (chorus)
I'm tired of this fight
With me is where you belong
But you never stay too long (all)

You're afraid of real love
You love me

You need me but you don't want me
I can't make you want me (chorus)
No one can make you want me
Have you ever? (all)
Have you ever been *in* love with me?

I need you, boy
You're the one I yearn for
No one (all)
I mean no one compares to you
You are my only one
The one I sure do love (chorus)
With whom I'm in love

But I'm leaving you, boy
Bid you farewell (all)
Don't call me anymore
Fly away from here, boy (chorus)
I'm moving to another country, boy
I don't want you to find me, boy (chorus)
I'm tired; so very tired of being your toy (all)
You've hurt me for the last time

Good bye
2007 (Song)

Suspenseful Passion

Rewind the tapes
Please
Listen to them again
You have the right to know

Know how I feel
Exactly
I said it
Now I'll say it again

I feel
For you
I love you
I need you
I care
Caring so much
I've lost touch
Touch with reality
Maybe this is reality
It is our reality

This is so real
So true
You've unlocked what's inside of me
Many have tried
But have failed

Something inside of you
Infuriated something inside of me
This is how we became

Turning time into gold
A platinum ring you gave me
Told me that you were marrying me
Can't see yourself with anyone else

You are my future
Knowing all of me
Every single bit
Titillating
Go to sleep
Catch some Zs
Baby bees
Please

I'm in love with you
Only you
The man I want to marry
We're so similar
You've touched me
Bewitched me
Body and soul

You're like an old gospel hymn
You move me
Tears and smiles at the same time
The music you give me
I hear melodies
I write them down in my head

There you are lying in bed
Fast asleep you went

I took good care of you
When you came in last night
Your feet were tired and your body was sore
I rubbed you down
Head to toe with body oil
I fed you pieces of passion fruit
Passion unbridled you gave in return
To me

Why do you love me?
1:06 AM 12/31/2006

Chapter One: Love

The Second Hiatus

Where Are You?

I haven't talked to you
Not at all
Not today
Which was actually yesterday

It's as though someone stole
My heart away
Did they take you?
I could care less
No need to stress
I'm your one and only lady

This is so unfair
I'm getting gray hairs
It feels as the day of the dinosaur
Time has gone by so slowly
Seamlessly
I call to you
But there's no answer
Maybe I allowed the phone to ring
Twice

Only
I know you hate it when I do that
Why do I do that?
I'm almost afraid of you
I've never been infatuated with you
I'm irreversibly in love with you

And I love you
My one and my only
Man you are
Reaching for the stars
We are

Taped live
Sparkling flies
I hate flies
They are so weird

Let's go straight to our happy ending
Baby, you know I
That I can surely die
Die without you
Simply
I need you
As the stars need the sky
I
Need you

Number nine
12:42 AM 12/27/06

Forever Your Lady

Happy is such an understatement
Ooh, oh
What to do?

Swimming and singing
Hidden thoughts
Of love
Grow old with me
Our true love is
Honestly, virtually, conceptually
True

All I have
Is for you
Well you know
I was blue
Before you
Am now you
Guided by this

This temptation
Rivers flow
Guide me
Your lady forever
The smell of the summer heat

It was raining yesterday
Sweet succulent scents of caramel
Pass me
Lowering myself down
Ready for the sight of you
6:04 PM 12/26/06

Because You Renovated My Heart

If I could I would give you my heart
This I'd do so we'd never part
For me this is very hard
I do not know how to share my heart
It has been broken before
Now it is thousands of non-restored pieces posing as one

What if it stops beating?
When does the two inevitably become one?
And which one is the dominant one?
The one that was hurting or the one that was unknowing?
I don't want my former hurt to overtake your present joy
I can't do that to you

What you can do is ignore me
Little 'ol me
That hurt *been* went away
On the day you came
1:32 AM 5/27/07

Development Issues

What's here for you?

The torch of flame
I am carrying

Laptop has been broken
I write *way* too often
Only way to reach me
Is through space and time
Unreliable

I
Search for you
What have I given?
Blue and green linen

Redeem yourself
Don't be under 29 when you die
I give you my heart
It's scarred

Is your name Brooks?

Life and heat
Stuffing with gravy
Flavored tenderly

My nose is so very sore
Blown for the last 24
The numbers won't leave the display

Music
Hesitantly keeps play
Take your vitamins
Wash your hair *and* my hair

In the night
I
Look for dreams
Real frosty

You owe me five dollars
I'll *take* a quarter

Develop yourself
Be understanding
I'm not your family
Ok

This is the real world
Earn it
Be serious
Stop modeling
Are you reading?

Do you have an apartment?
See you tomorrow with the records

Surprise
Surprise
Rent an apartment
Who is Vahnessia?
Her name is strange
Beautiful people

Your money is good
Only here
Hand carved wood
Shavings
Hanging around the top

See you real soon
No exceptions
Pink stockings on
I am good
Where are my things?

It is unfurnished
One room
Take up your things
Are you lying to me?
$1800 in the *whole*

I saw you run into the pole
Car insurance is high
Where is your agent?
Cigars and smoke
Don't want to choke
Do you have an appointment?

I'll make you out to be a judge
And *I'll* judge that
Lean back
No pictures
Get some prints done

Travel to Paris
Don't be dishonest
1:53 AM 12/28/06

I Wonder Why

I see that you called today
I wonder why
You never call
Well, you hardly call
You called because you see that I *didn't* call you

Oh, fickle can you be
Calling me
Reaching out to me
Because I didn't call you
Sometimes you treat me bad
You treat me like a cancer
Wondering why

I sitting here high
You not knowing
That I love you
So deep in love with you
"Huh?"
Maybe next time around

You'll think of me
Call me *maybe*
Wow
This is so crazy
Dysfunctional
You are

I like pretty things
What's wrong with that?
A diamond in the rough
That's what you are
I *should* have picked gold
Well

What should I do?
What ought I say?
I didn't even talk to you today
Now my back hurts
I worked so hard
I did it for you
I had you in mind

Why don't you ask me things?
I should have never dated you
And it's so close to the holidays

Be like yourself
I don't want you to be like everyone else
You went so far away
"So, *Merry Christmas*"
That's all I want to say
You won't call me anyway

I don't ask for much
I ask you for nothing
Not ever
Not once
Wait and see

Come back
Where are you going?
Why are you floating?
Your mind is so not here to stay
You already went away

Silence now
Be quiet
Be still
I'm always
Always
Thinking of you
It makes me stressed
I need a massage
On my wish list
Dreams come true
11:58 PM 12/22/06

Long Distance Love

Today was awesomely beautiful
It was Christmas Day
There was so much love in the air
I spent it with my family

My dear was far away
But not *too* far away
He called me
He was so sweet and so kind

Simply the way I love him
He is *my* baby
I wish I could see him
I keep his picture close

Close to my bed
The place where I lay my head
My head at night
In there I dream
I dream of tender kisses
Kisses good and true
Only to be received from him

He gently holds my hand
Squeezes down on my palm
My fingers embrace him

Oh, to say goodbye
There I'd die

Where is my daddy?
There he is
Take me
Away from here
This man wishes to marry
He said he is marrying only me
Oh, how could this be?

I don't deserve him
Or *do* I?

Baby boy
Oh, baby boy
Marry me please
You are younger than I
And I don't care
You worship so well
Loving God on high

Come sit down
Let me make sure
You are fine
You've influenced me
Like a child
Making me want to be better

When I look into your eyes
I simply see me looking back
At me
You've become me
And I've become you
We are one
Talk to me

We're in love
Don't you know?
I'm never leaving your side
I can't believe you are here

Why do you stay?
With me
I'm far from faultless
Can't you see?
I'm quite off-centered

Before you there was one
He only *needed* me
Never wanted me
He used me
He left me
I was purely hurt

Oh, but *now* I'm so glad
Very glad
You are here
Here to stay
Well, that's what you say
Man, you've sure made my day

No way

I want you forever
And a day
11:19 PM 12/25/06

True Love Penetrated

I never meant to harm you
Never meant to lie
It was just that I

I was afraid to be wanted by you
Afraid of what could be
You made me
Forced me
To be the real me
Where I was, *was* forbidden
I *don't* let anyone in here
Not even me
You came in

You came in with me
It didn't hurt
Not one bit
How I fell for you is this

My heart was pricked
You shot straight through the skin
And my skin is thick
Thicker than thick
You saw me standing all alone
Talking on the phone
With someone I don't know

It's been awhile now
I wouldn't talk to you
Seemed like it had to go your way
A man I wasn't looking for
Only wanted to be left alone

Hadn't been hurt in awhile
For this I was happy
It was two years almost three
Of being essentially free

Men try to hold on to me
But I ask them to let go
"Let go of me"
Don't want to be held
I'm my own
Own to run and be me
Lingering free
Wild horses run beside me

This lovely lady
Crossing my legs
With my petite hands to accompany them
Long locks of reddish brown hair flowing
Down my back
Looks like a pretty singing bird
I wanted to be free
You came and rescued me
Rescued me from *me*

Calm and settled
No longer on the run
Nor afraid of love
Now belonging to you
Cocoa butter heals
Scars that is
You showed me, me
From *inside* of me
I actually let you in

What's wrong with me?
Allowing a man to catch up with me
Well, you were in front of me
Walking beside me now
For this I wear a smile
Cultivated and chosen
3:55 AM 1/01/07

Away

I miss you, baby
I miss you like crazy
It's only been a few days since we've went away but it hurts me
Hurts like crazy

Have I ever told you that I love you?
Well, I do
I do still
I always will
I always have

Days flow by ever so gently
I hear the hummingbirds singing songs
They are love songs
The songs we both enjoy

We've shared so much love throughout the years
Now, we've parted
We've gone separate ways
You reside in a different state that I
It's killing me inside
I'm coming to where you are

You are my family
True family lives on in one's heart
A long time ago you gave me your heart
I often wondered why

With you I have security
A reason for breathing
A reason for simply being

I've held your hands through many trials people put you through
I've been Lois Lane for you
Never would I nor have I allowed someone to hurt you

Send all snakes to me
I'll take care of your problems
That is how much I care

You complete me
You have protected me
And guarded me from outside pain
Now that you're gone
I don't know what I'll do

I'm coming for you
Where you are is where my heart belongs
Come back to me
How can you just leave me?
You didn't leave me with a sign
You took this tearful heart of mine
You asked me *if* I wanted to follow
But I wished you would have stayed

Now I must leave this place
It reminds me of you
The scent of you
The millions of memories that I hold of you
They haunt in the middle of the night
I can't sleep
I continuously cry and cry
My eyes are as huge as casaba melons
The water ducts are drying up quickly

What should I ever do?
Maybe
Just maybe
I should get over you
Move on with my life
If you wanted me you would have stayed
Or you would have took me with you
Why can't you come to where I am?

Life without pictures of you is useless
If my memory serves me correctly
You asked me to take on anything you could throw at me
I took on *everything* and yet you left

Fish and jelly bellies
Honeysuckles
Amber fields
Mountain plains
Heartaches unmistakably grey
The pain in my head
Down to my feet and toes
Back up to my gentle, precious heart
How much more sensitive can I be?

Oh, silly me
Believing truly, wholeheartedly that you'd really, eventually stay with me
You have me
Body, mind, heart, and soul
What else can I give?
I could give you *me*
But do you want me?

As you walked away
Tears streamed down my caramel face
Time stood still
The sweetest kiss I could ever give wasn't sweet enough
You still left
Yet I have your heart
I know beyond a shadow of a doubt that you love me

You left
I'm coming
I'm coming right behind you
180 days into 180 degrees
I love you; yes, I do
Blue bonnets and yellow daisies
I still hear those hummingbirds
Those kind love songs
You sang them to me

When will you get me from the airport?
2:42 PM 5/9/07

A Year Gone By

I enjoyed yesterday
I almost hate to see it go
It is a *pass* year
So we look on to the new one to come

Yesterday you gave to me
Yourself unrestrained

You didn't rush me
You kept calling me
Did exactly what you said
You rarely break your promises
For this I'm glad

With you I'm never sad
You fill me up
Joy comes from God
He sent me you
Look at the peace I'm in
Oh, joy
Joy

You are not a boy
All man
Old things are passed away
Happy New Years!
3:00 AM 1/01/07

Chapter One: Love

The Third Hiatus

The Truth Is

It is so crazy
I said I love you
I did mean you
So scary it seemed
To finally be open about some things

I was so excited I could have burst
But I became simple and shy
Felt I was going to cry
Maybe even I was going to die

I opened up
Did I?
Oh, me
Oh, my
Shoot my eye
Was it real?
Maybe
Why?
It may push you away
So I'll take it back
I don't mean it
Act like I never said it
Clear your head of it
Why did I say such a thing?
Maybe I meant it
You make me smile
Internally
Externally
Globally
So much that I cry
Being awfully to blind

Give me life
Caring for me
For real with all honesty
Adoring me
Laughing at my stupid jokes
I whispered softly then stoked
Wore that crazy purple coat
Chunky noodle toes
Using only green and blue soap
Drive a hot pink Chevrolet Corvette that used to be gold and taupe
Never did dope

You like me just for me
This really
And could be
The one and only

Man for me
Said I love you
Blah! Did I?
Oh, me
Oh, my
I never lied
I tried

You know me
You caught me
Looked into my soul
Where did you come from?
I never looked for you
Nor did I call you
You've captured my soul
Without a doubt
You win
You truly do
Because
I
Love
You
3:36 AM 1/01/07

Without Drama

You're the one that I want
Now, you know this and *unfortunately*, so do everyone else
You knew it from the start
Stole my heart
Took it right away
What was *something* you wanted to say?

Have I ever been the one?
The one you can't breathe without
The one you love without a doubt
I never want to cause you hurt
No pain
No sorrow

Love me
At *least*
'Til tomorrow

Hold me tight
Wrap me up
Keep your tender hands on me
Fragile
I am
Draw nigh to me
Tell me
You need me
I'm flexible and willing to compromise
I'm such a lady
Never swear, curse, or drink
I have not caused you drama

You imagined me as your child's mama
And *not* without the ring
It could even be a plastic ring
Sealed with a kiss
I give of myself wholeheartedly to you
I don't want to run
Not away
Away from you
We may run together
Run on
Into the moon light
I'm here to make you feel better
Here to be your help
Your soul mate
Simply royalty
9:40 PM 1/02/07

Futuristic Brilliance

Now it's time for bed

There's been enough said
Sweet thoughts of you rummage through my head
Hopefully, you're not afraid by what I said

You've never been in love
Not before me
Well, what if we?
No, no
Not us
How could this be?
I can't allow you to capture me
What if you fell in love with me?
What would it mean for me? *We*?
They'd try to break us up
Wouldn't they?
Could they?
No, not us
We'd make a fuss

You are beautiful
That's an understatement
Don't look at me like that
We need a yacht
To get away
And plot

Plot out our future
It's so clear
It is evident
We are one
Walking
Talking
Being the *ones*
We're taking things over

Positivism for them
Ah, for us
We can't help that we are strong
We're number one

Can't get me away from your heart
I'm going to barf
Think you're smart?
Intelligent?
We'll see

Baby, it's me
Only me
Come here
So we

We can go to the park

Sit under a willow tree in the dark
Hold my hand
Intellectuals are we
Yes, we are

You've been placed by me
Together we make an awesome pair
Hand in hand
This plan is so cool
Nothing to lose
Someone's in our corner
Me *4* you
You for me
Constantly
Thank you
You're the best to me
I believe in you, honey
Sugar pie, honey lump
No way *I'd* ever dump
Trash on you or around you
King of my kingdom
Queen of your castle
I'm there
For you

You see
Loving you
Needing me
Honey bee
Sugar cones
Maple scones
Tasty to me

Brighter days ahead
Futures so bright
Need double protection shades
One for you
One for me
Together we…
4:13 AM 1/01/07

Ordained For You

Yes
Yes
I'll marry you
On which day?
I'd marry you any day
Any day that you say

You are my love
My dear heart
From you I'll never part
Put the eggs and grits in the cart
Let me play my part
I give you all of my heart

You love mashed potatoes
I'll make you some of those
To be in love with me
Saying you need me
"Oh, wee"
Going to the movies
Climbing mountain peaks
I love to hear you speak

I've prayed for you
Today
Yesterday

Play that trombone
Flute
Strings
Buenos noches, senor

Smiling at me with that grin
It's so unreserved
No teeth showing
Slight dimples protruding
Eyes gazing at me
You never take them off of me
Gorgeous, I am
A lady always
Prissy
Highly sophisticated
Dressed to the *T*

There you go looking at me
Wanting me
Come to me
I told you yes

Yes
Yes
Never a no
Nor a maybe
Yes's only

I've only had the best
You are thee best
Best dressed
Classical
Well refined
Gentleman at all times

Caring for me
I'm here to help you
Give into me
You alone
It wasn't hard to do
You were made first
God ordained

I'm marrying you
You asked me to
I was afraid of you
You didn't have to steal my heart
I gave it freely to you
I deserve you
Together we soar
2:54 AM 1/01/2007

You Give Me Cheerful Cries

There's a tear in my eye
It stems from the memory of the day that you came into my life
It hasn't been real easy but it sure hasn't been that hard
I think of your smile and I cry
You say I make you happy
Oh, my

XM Radio

I must admit
I allowed you to win
You win
Won by that grin

I continuously close my eyes
Crying *while* I kiss you
This is too real
Way too real
Could it be true?
The love for me
You
Give it always
Do

Hearing music
Everywhere
They don't believe it's true
I've never cared
Before you
I sang songs of
Unreal things

The thought of us being is simply
Impossible
Liking me just the way I am
You don't ask me for much
Never asked me for a thing
Just to show my true feelings

I haven't a clue
I do this to you
Open my heart

I will
Let you in
Give you what I've got
Giving you more
Explore
Close the door

Man of war
Not physical
Not verbal
Of *love*
You've conquered
Won
The untamable me

You deserve me
Took the time to get to know me
Know me better than I know myself
Took my heart off of the shelf
Opened the world's door to me
Spiritually
Musically
6:38 PM 12/26/06

Unbreakable

Good night, my dear
For you there is no substitute
You've made me so very happy
You called me '*hott*'
I didn't notice
We talked a lot

Distance and miles
Quite far away, not even close
The man I love and need the most
Laughing at me
Frequently
Causing me to smile

Not often do I cry
Tears of happiness and joy
Overwhelming joy
Joys of love
It's like scrap iron
We're unbreakable
Thin yet undeniably strong

It's like a surprise given to Mrs. Wesley on The Cosby Show after the baby arrived
You cause for me to have tears in my eyes
Laughs
And laughing
At the thought of you
The way you love me
You've never denied me

I hear the baby crying
My sister's daughter
She was asleep
Turn off the TV
Nope
Switch over to a channel named *Bulah*
New and unrated
Redesign of station 9
It's now channel 5
Not making sense
Am I?
1:37 AM 12/28/06

Visions Of The Sea

Open your heart
Let your love flow down
I am beneath you with every move you make
Trees run free when the earth shakes
Crumbles of sharp leaves swirl through the air
Time has been suspended because you're near

Oh where have I gone?
Where have I run to?
Longing to be beside you is always there
Carefully I whisper
I part my mouth to say
"I want you"
Show me the way

Time has stood still in this same place for me
Have you seen me here?
What to do now?
What happens next?
Tall as a mountain my breasts heap dances of joy
There is a man that finds me where ever I go
He touches my love so gently and swims away

It is in the land
All around you and me
Juices flow down my thigh
Simply to hit the earth
The earth is green and free to love all

Waters of the river run far and long
The night air is so cool
And I looked for you
You *were* no where to be found
Actually you were blue
Blue as the crisp Australian Sea
Coast guards looked high and low
Yet couldn't find me
And I couldn't find *you*
Because you were in my heart
I had been carried away by the sea
9/19/06

Foreseen Memories

These are the memories
That makes a melody
A piece of time
Here, I
Think of you
What you do
Do to me
You walk pass me
Ignore me
Return my call
Not right after

What's happening?
I turn right back
Back into you
Place my *cora* courage
Honor
With you

Prove yourself
Why should I stay?
Once called me beautiful
Now you look at me all mad
The tears I've cried
Drowned me in a river
My voice now fades
There is some sunshine
But a smell of rain

Songs by Jon Bon Jovi
I don't regret this life
I live in the water
My spirit swims free
Everyday
Thunder road
Freedom valley
9:58 PM 5/02/07

You Did

In you I lost myself
In you I found myself
In this soul search I found myself and a little bit more
It was a race against time
I prayed it *rage*
It almost was a frightening ending
I made you release me
You didn't want to
This is a tradition for me
I'll never stay
Don't try to make me

When I get to the other side I'll let you know I made it
Don't try to visit me there
Don't you dare
I hate loving you
Loving you leaves me in full despair
Loving you, in honesty is truly unfair
I gave you my heart
I gave you my love
I held strongly to my soul
For you attempted to steal it from me

You loved me once
Once is not enough
11:35 AM 4/07/07

Keeping It Real

Inside there is hurt
There is pain
What are you in this to gain?

All I feel is emptiness
My face is flush
Ideally, I am not the natural choice
I was so impossible

It was difficult to be with you
Uncertainty had crept in
Only because you were a young man

Where was the honesty?
It had given me some modesty
Such a *test* dealing with me
You had passed
Quite well
Surprisingly to me

You are *close* to fail
Now you've pushed me aside
Deep inside I cry
Never would I
Have allowed someone to get to me
I'm not from the *streets*
Never wanted to be

Etiquette; hands down
Perfection of quality
What a lady *ought* to be
You treat me unfairly
I give so much to you
Opened my dear heart up for you
When you call you never say "baby"
My lady
Fair lady

Instead I have to bare down to hear you say
"Hey, man"
"Yo, buddy"
Who are they?
You owe me
More than that
You know me best
So why must I constantly guess?
Who and what I am to you
Am I or am I not your lady?
So close you *are*
To losing me
2:51 PM 1/03/06

A Rendezvous To Remember

You made it very clear how you felt
You are a victim of this political society
You refuse to lead your way to *your* future
You follow in another's footsteps
What confusing decisions you make
You behave like a senile old man
You don't deserve me
Actually, you never did

Our friendship hangs on *un-bountiful* tidings
Sitting in front of me are the letters you sent me
Each one was read and reread
Our alliance is over
Your saddened words were *mistakably* strong
Not strong enough to keep me
Beads of pain race up my back
I gave you something good

Austere expressions settle on my once pleasant face
Looks from you remind me of breeched *rackets*
The languages of our romance dwindles away
Today on this peculiar eve I run free
I can't make it to our meeting
Looks like its going to happen

A plane is waiting just for me at the airport
Finally and all at once
I'm leaving
11:17 PM 4/12/07

Losing You

Don't smile at me
Don't even try
It is time that we
Say goodbye

If it's me
Then it's me
Let me go
Let me be

I wanted to be me
I always wanted to be me
What do you want from me?
Why do you even trust me?
Love has no place here
Let it run down

The ants go marching
Two by two
"Hooray!"

I want to leave
I need to go
Keep me near you
Stand close
Pull me in
Dearly touch me
Feed me
Be with me
I need you
I wanted to belong to you
That's all
I'm amazed by you

They came to take me away

Why didn't you follow?
You didn't even bother
They made me an offer
An offer to turn you in
I wouldn't do that
I'd never tell your secrets
I need a pen
I'll write you
And tell you want they wanted to hear
Turn my baby in
"No way!"
Not here

Generally, I long for you
But not on today
They came
They took me away
I dare not say
That I didn't care to stay
Not to stay with you that is

You gave up on me a long time ago
Now I must go
Why do you do this so?
You may have never loved me
My soul is connected to you
But you left me
Not physically
Mentally
Spiritually
Why?
Oh, why?
I need you

I'm crying
Take me
Connect with me
Baby?
I'm losing it
I'm losing you
12:30 AM 12/22/06

No Idea

The woman that was murdered out by the sea has *no* idea of what I am going through
Everything started happening when I fell in love with you
My life is great and full of our space
You understand me and know me thoroughly and it's great
But do you love me?
Love me as a wife and not as a typical spouse
There is a difference

To be a wife I would be your other half
The other side of you
The one to make you laugh
I would wipe away your tears when you cry
I'd love you no matter *what* happened to you on the outside
You are truly beautiful to me from inside out
Why can't you just stay in love with me?

If you looked at me as wife you'd see these true things
The scrumptious meal I cooked for you *when* I was tired as hell
The new suit I saw you eye in Bloomingdales
I had it tailored to fit your body the way you like it
I left you the sweetest message on your voicemail when I felt that you were having a rough work day
Your face was aglow when you walked through the door
I lay down on our living room couch for you to only find your best surprise
A box of your favorite chocolate wrapped in crimson red paper

I want to be the one to pick you up when you are feeling down
To love you through all eternity
They say that love lasts forever
I have my doubts on that and I do not find it to be true
Forever has a time limit on it
Forever is *only* available during one's existing lifetime
But when I die my love for you will be as always
I will always love you
While I am here and when I am gone
For this I am sure

Knowing you is so splendid

How could I love another?
I want to be blue
I'd be blue so I could mix in with the ocean and the sea
I'd lie there awake until I found you
If I were ever to lose you oh what would I do?

I slept there at your feet when you were sick
I never left your side
Even in your sickness you are strong
I gain strength from you just *knowing* that you keep my safe from all alarms
Somewhere or someday someone took your love away
You are the greatest man and I want to stand by my man
What took your love from me?
What could it possibly be?
Why do you now hate me?

My heart and soul belongs to you and you alone
I would die for you if you asked me to
I find myself quite often staring out into empty spaces and blank faces
I am so delusional now because you took your love away
You treat me bad and then beg me to stay
You said that you need me
You protect me from everything harmful but not from you
The most harmful thing in my life
That's what you are

You have my heart and it was once right
With my heart being outside of my soul I have no where to go
So I need you to lead me
I trust you so
Don't leave me
Say that you believe in me
As I do you

You are running a race that you know that you can win but know that you ought not to
You used to *not* cheat, lie, and steal but you changed to accommodate others
You once changed for me too
And you changed on me
You left me but you are yet *still* here
Why not leave me?
Take your heart
I don't want it anymore

I love you always
I said it before but I now need you to close my door
You let in this grave chill when you entered in
Where did it come from?
You once were a changed and reformed man
I helped you all that I can and I got hurt in the end
The process was smooth and easy; never annoying
You made me crazy and you made me brave
I was glad and proud to be your lady

You took your love away, dear baby
The woman that was murdered out by the sea has *no* idea of what I am going through
Why can't she see?
3:30PM 3/20/2007

It Could Be Pernicious

You seem to be so forlorn without my love
I sure wonder what happened
It's a natural thing for an unloved woman to leave the place where she had lived in shame
It's a very hard thing to do but it can be done
I left and found useful *employment*
I looked directly through my heart and found you hiding deep down inside
I ask you now
"Are you well?"

This is the most bizarre tiding I've ever took part in
It is a true disaster
You say no to give me your heart but decline to depart from my soul
My soul will by no means belong to anyone else besides you
But this time I'm a fool
This is so untoward so please excuse me
I'll say this only once then I'm gone
"I *hate* to love you"

We are tangled up in an unyielding maze of desire
Since you long to listen to them, go *stay* with them
You can be at no lost as to why I am here
I long to recover my spirit from you
Do not ask to marry me again
The thought is unfathomable
2:40 PM 5/18/07

Not Today

Should've, would've, could've
But I didn't
That's what I tell myself
I should have left when I thought of it but I wasn't actually *thinking*
I would have left but you held onto my hand
I could have run but I didn't; my feet wouldn't move
I didn't leave
I hate to go
And I wonder what your secrets are

You left me
You went away
It's almost as you *wanted* to leave
You wanted to leave me
Time flies and passes away
Today was almost the day
It could have been a good day
I'm missing you so much
Missing you like crazy
You don't call me
You don't call me at all
I hate the fact that you don't care
You could care less
Everything is just a mess
I love you so much
Others couldn't even compare

Do you still want me?
Do you think of me?
You simply just don't care
I think of you constantly
I hurt so much that I *can't* cry
Not even a little
A tear comes into the corner of my eye
Turns a U and goes back
My tears say "take me away"

You were a gift from above
To simplify things
I need you to go away
Stay away from here
Stay away from me
You have not masterminded the *idea* of me
I am a reality
Pure and true
Heaven opened its arms once to welcome you
My love is free
What about yours?
You wouldn't know
You've never loved
Never do you stop to think
Not about me
You are way too serious
Too serious with yourself

Stop calling me
Oops, you already did
It's a pity and it's a shame
I would have had your kid
The lovely blue dress you bought
Just to wear for you is dead
The *dress* has no life
You are not here
You don't want to
Don't want to be here
Not with me
I'm frustrated and blue
Blue like that dress
The one I would wear
Just for you
Let me watch you grow
My love has been interrupted
Why do you do this so?
Basically you do not care
Here goes that tear again
Right now I must summon up a good laugh
I have to force this feeling to pass

Spontaneity is great
But frequency is even better
Frequently concern yourself with me
Am I safe?
Am I breathing?
Well, that's that
Feels like you hit me with an old baseball bat
I counted to five
"Five" *they* say
That's the way
I wanted to be with you

As days grew by
Not once
Not even
Didn't you give it a try?

"Humor" *they* say
Yeah, that's the way
You are so funny
I forgot to laugh
"Ha!"
Thanks for the laugh
Your time was well spent
"Not!"
Recount the times you looked for me
1, 2, that's it
Your jig is up
Partner
We could have been great partners
I give 100 percent
You give 100 percent
I taught you that

I glance at your picture
Everyday
"Everyday" I say
I look and listen
For what it has to say
You sent no messages
Not today
Never
You only call when you want something
It's crazy because you never called for *me*

Silver bells
Hear the bells
I hear them in my heart
They share the love
I count down the days
Slowly they go by

I ask myself
"Why can't I cry?"
It's like a movie
The plot
The climax
The resolution
And the end
Let's end it
End it now
I'm tired of being played
As a drum
Yet, I *don't* hate you

Not at all
Not today
12:01 AM 12/22/06

Forgiveness Of Disenchanted Calamity

Moving on
I'll find a way to forgive and forget you
The tattered pain that shoots through the core of my soul
My heart refuses to let go
I know that I need to
It's only right
Once you made me strong
Presently, you've accomplished to make me bitterly weak

It's been 37 weeks since this begun
The tainted love you give me
This has to be about forgiveness
It's good that I let go
I refuse to die over this
I will humble myself although I'm thoroughly humiliated
I must get down to the heart of the matter
I've cried so much that my voice is tampered
You don't love me any longer
I've seen this craziness stirring
Your embedment of someone else

Lamentably for me, I miss you at times
It's killing me inside
Yet you don't know
Just don't recognize
I'm forgiving you
I must go on
Forever, I love you
Just don't *yearn* for you anymore
My fatal bruises are over
My spirit is worn

You found someone; you let go of the things we once shared
The uninhibited devotion
The tears
The laughter
The places we went
The support
The memories

Although you don't love me anymore
There is this need of exoneration
Thus, I forgive
I've recovered my soul, so there's a way to move on
1:07 PM 6/04/07

Prejudices Of The Proud

The distance between us is killing me
I'm dying ever so slowly
My soul seeps away from my once vivacious body
I am bursting with life when you are close to me
When you are gone I weep

Oh, the affection I have for you
I look up to only find your face in the sky
Come home to me
Surely you must know that what I *do* is all for you?
I am out of my senses with you
My heart floats up on carriages
"I love you"
You are him
You don't really know what I am like
You've misjudged me
So have I *misjudged*?
I had misjudged you because of your indifferences

Once upon a time
We were so similar
Both so stubborn

You and I
We've strictly changed
I wish my mother could see me on today
I'm quite at my leisure
My prejudices have disappeared
No longer am I cantankerous anymore
Ode to Darcy
5/18/07

Chapter Two: Inspire

The First Hiatus

Axioms And Adages:

We waste time, our own time and other's by not knowing who we are or why we are. I do not want us to waste our time any longer by just *being* but now be in time *justifiably.*
2007

This dude once asked me why I am so difficult. I replied "I am not difficult nor am I complicated; I am just simply *unfooled-around-with*".
4/2007

I am infinitely invincible to be ultimately *invisible.*
2:46 PM 5/21/07

I once told you that I'd do anything for you. This *was* true. Now, I'll tell you that I'll do something for you. I'll open my door for you, honey, so you may get out! You've took enough from me. I not having you *am* possible to be without.
12:56 AM 5/27/07

Leave my heart at the door hurriedly for you're not welcomed nor invited anymore.
12:57 AM 5/27/07

I prepared for you a place of rest. You in *return* gave me a place of distress.
12:58 AM 5/27/07

There is a time when one finds his place in the sun. Bask in its glory. Don't turn back; look on towards your journey. It's a long road but it'll be a good story.
1:02 AM 5/27/07

Everyone has a degree of character. The question is do you have a *13* or an *88*?
6/08/07

I needed you to give me your heart. You did. I know this now. You told me you did and I felt it. Still, it is fabulously strange. Quite strange, indeed.
4/20/07

You are committed to me and don't even realize it; you love me yet you *won't* say it.
9:28 AM 3/05/07

Writing is true flabbergasted unsung, *then* re-released, deep thought words.
11:19 PM 5/17/07

I would have been a great proficient if I ever learnt how to love. I need the practice; *will* you take the time to show me?
1:54 PM 5/18/07

You had asked me to stay with you, to love you and to always be true. I heard everything that you said. Unfortunately, I can not stay. I guess two out of three in actuality isn't that bad?
2007

I'm at your disposal as long as you need me; just don't *dispose* of me.
1:58 PM 5/18/07

My heart is overjoyed with the way you love me most ardently. However, you've forever exposed my sacred feelings to the world by letting others know that you never actually *intended* to stay with me.
2:02 PM 5/18/07

Who can really know how much damage we've done to the earth? The once beautiful and fruitful subject screams out in sheer resound; "Stop". *Are* we listening?
2:07 PM 5/18/07

We listen in but do we truthfully have the sense of hearing what is being said? We *choose* to be deaf.
2:11 PM 5/18/07

He had such a handsome face; he whom saved my life. I do not know his name nor do I care to remember. All to consider is the fact; he had saved my life. Now without a doubt I can not stop smiling *about.*
2:14 PM 5/18/07

He met her once, then once again and this time he promised not to let her go as he did one time before. So why does he continue to sit so *closely* to the door?
2:15 PM 5/18/07

One day you will turnaround and notice me for the first time. Hundreds, even thousands of times you've fixed your eyes upon my face yet you've never actually *seen* me.
2:20 PM 5/18/07

I have hope. Hope in grave situations. Expenditures of some sort I have to give. They can not buy anyone's way out but surely great faith can.
2:22 PM 5/18/07

Yes, I am passionately committed, but I do not take myself seriously; I'd laugh at that. Truly.
10:19 AM 5/25/07

I refuse to be a celebrity; who in actuality wants to be the center of attention? I despise superficial attention.
10:23 AM 5/25/07

Love is a choice; I choose not to love you anymore for your lack of consistency in loving me back.
11:13 AM 5/25/07

I'm trying to find a way to forgive you for what you've done; so I'll unbolt my heart from this floor because if I don't *we'll* die from this pain I feel inside.
3:57 PM 6/03/07

I have a paper cut. And oh, snaps! I almost died. I'm a lady. I can't lose my life. *Bandages?*
11:20 PM 6/10/07

I see that you possess a 4.0 GPA in your scholastic education but frankly you are a *spot on idiot box* when it comes to personality.
12:05 AM 6/11/07

I've always had something to say to you but lately, I just become silent; silent to the fact that you are not listening.

10:12 PM 5/08/07

This is me. This is what I've got. This is what I'm giving. This is what you'll get and that's it. What else do you want? Your want is *your* master.
12:11 AM 6/17/07

The Way To Me

Extend me, please
Respect me, please
Love me, please
Honor me, please
Remain loyal to me
Trust me
8:20 PM 5/31/07

A Letter To College Friends:

Hello, my friends. **I miss all of you,** especially the ones that have recently graduated. Good luck to all of you! Make the best of what you've got and get more of what you want. Be who you were born to be. "Lean not to your own understanding but in all thy ways acknowledge Him." Bible

I'm writing today to say that this summer will be what we make it; our lives are what we make them. *Unfortunately*, we all only have ONE life to live so I wish everyone the best (even my enemies). I love you guys! If it weren't for our enemies we wouldn't be who we really should be. We would be good but would we be **great**? I'm not sure. I don't even think so. Those who hate me <u>inevitably</u> make me stronger. They make me study a little more. They make me run a little faster. They make me love my man deeper. And they make me dream harder. And that is bona fide determination!

Haters hate what you love to make you feel as though something is not real or that something is unattainable. Ha! I must love that antic. Their hatred is a force to be reckoned with. "I reckon that you are an idiot in the purest form." My life is an elevator and I am moving up and out. If you are not on it for the right reasons or if you are trying to ride the elevator down then 'get off'! I'm not the one and never will be.

If you know you have the right friends be their umbrella. Stick by them no matter what! Friends are the people you **choose** to have in your world. You have **no** choice of family (laugh out loud!). Pray for those you know; they may seem to be on Easy Street but they have a way of coping with things and they do not let you know. I love my friends they are respectable young men and women. I choose my friends by their standing. Is he a gentleman? Is she a lady?

Make sure your friends' motives are right (check people's reasoning for having their time in your circle). Are they moving in the right direction? Or are they moving in your direction to steal *your* dream? Some people are here for a reason, some a season, and some a lifetime. We are in school to get our education and to learn of ourselves. Have you checked your reasons lately for being here? This is the summertime and for those taking courses I congratulate you. Those who are not I congratulate you as well for surveying this vast world of possibilities.

There is so much to do. Travel. Visit family. Visit friends. Read a classic. Go to the movies. Catch a play. Go bowling. Run around the amusement park. Go swimming. Meet and make new acquaintances. Get a new hair style. Paint a picture. Tell your man/woman how you 'really' feel. If it is not what's best for you, then leave. I hate seeing people unhappy. If it is what is best for you then stay and make it work. Be pleasantly overjoyed. Make a reservation at a wonderful restaurant and bask in your favorite entree'. Rearrange your room/home. Clean out your closet. **Dream a new dream**.

"And because God is the greatest power, we shall never be defeated!" Bible

If I ever offended <u>any</u> of you **please** accept my apologies.

We must stop living in the dead zone.

I really need for you to love yourself...
5/2007

72

Where Friends Are

Friends are the greatest
At least mine are anyway
They stay and listen to me fret during the day
We wash and blow-dry one another's hair even at the latest hours of the night

Friends are dear and real friends are true
They try their best and darnedest not to cause harm and anguish to you
My friends have pride and show sympathy
They are inquisitive, smart, and beautiful
They can be quite hilarious, comical, and supportive
Never do you turn your back on a friend

When you want to please any one of them you show them your illustrious grin and say "I made my famous baby back ribs"
Smiles and giggles always resound from my *hills*
Love is a fine thing and it is contagious
To have and retain friends you must first be a friend
I dearly appreciate my friends
They stick close to me and me them
Never should someone try to annoy any one of them
If they do I am right there to the rescue
Don't mess with me for I am a force to be reckoned with
Balls of fire shoot from my lovely brown eyes
The sky stops circulating for me to gather space and time

A true friend's heart could calm a raging storm
Ask me how I know?
I've done it before
Why do people choose to get in the way of a community?
Why choose the option to destroy camaraderie?
Some are miserable
Some are untrue
Some have nothing else to do besides walking around being dramatically blue

A friend knows when you need them
A friend knows when you are on your way
A friend knows when there is a cloudy day on its way and sends you a card that says 'sunshine is on the way'
Friends give you peace, joy and something to hope for
When your friend is in love so are you
You become so elated and optimistic because you know it can happen for you too

Friends share their *last* Aquafina with you and if you seem to be hungry they donate their peaches and cream oatmeal too
Friends are great but they are rare
Look around
Take out some time
Are they there?

If not they are on their way
Be patient and have a great day

You can ask a friend to go with you to the pet store and they will go even if they are afraid of cats
When you have a friend you learn how to sacrifice
You learn how to give back
Life isn't all about you but they share your world too
It is what makes life so great
Having not enough food really but sharing what's on the plate

I believe in my friends because they are bold and sometimes dumb enough to believe in me
And my thousands of fanciful dreams
Sometimes we do things that we not ought
Why do we stick around and get disappointed?
Why *did* I lie that time and know that I'd get caught?
My friend stole my apple pie but that's alright
We stay because we have hope
We hope that people will change
And if they are a friend they usually do
3:59PM 3/20/07

Idiotic Exertion Of You And Your Entourage

At first I thought you hated me
Because of the way you treated me
Nowadays I realize that you adore me
Unbeknownst to yourself
It is my time
Listen

I do not change
For I am who *I* wish to be
I used to be thin skinned
Now my skin is *thick*
Almost incapable of penetration
I've heard them speak of me
Negatively
"Ha!"
I laugh

I love this
These words they give and even on times
It's been you

They tried to hurt my core
I only tried more
At first I wanted to be a writer
But after all the pains and struggles
I added on two occupations more
I do not succeed for the mere being of me
I rush forward to aid someone like you
Take time to comprehend who you are
Do not worry about me
I made it to the front line
I fought in countless wars

You continue to hide behind those 'supposed' friends of yours
They are quite phony and untrue
Continuously perpetrating frauds and putting on facades
What about me?
I *remain* true
I was pushed out the back then down
I was sent out to survive on my own
I wasn't sought after
I wasn't considered necessary anymore
"Ha!"
I laugh once more
The ones who hard-pressed me
Are *now* banging down my door

I glanced out the window
I looked
I saw
Exactly, I *knew* I heard your pathetic voice
3:31 PM 6/03/07

Whispering In The Dark

75

There are voices
Ones only heard in the dark
They continuously whisper and tear lives apart
Be careful of who you love
They may turn you in when times get hard
Dollars and pennies add up
Given of everything *once* needed

Where do you work?
What do you do?
There is a recreation taking place
Doing lab work brings about millions of answers
Everything is in its place
Frustrated to find a conclusion
It is a criminal investigation
There's the body that was found
Can you still hear the whispering in the dark?
1:26 PM 5/14/07

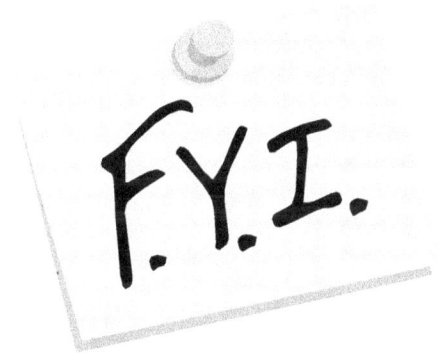

Truth Imposters

Some news is old news
Stop toting it around
Why do we choose to mind others business?
It is not ours to know
Snooping around in what is not ours is a dangerous affair

Clouds settle far below the skyline
We all have answers
Not answers that can be used
Who is on call?
Some wish to come back
Everything that has a beginning has an end
The beginning's not far back

If you fight to win
Let the games begin
Look through glasses just to be followed by *vacant* dust

Those that have been here before

There are bad men
Don't get to know them
Their hate affects the soul
Do what you are *meant* here to do

Years of non-servitude rendering only *one* moral fiber
Seek the truth
There is a revolution
Familiarity breeds condescension

At the sound of the hand striking down it'll be 7 o'clock
Make a clear cut decision
The facts of your society's survival
Hangs in the balance
It is best that everyone not deduce vigilance
Die for your cause if it's a *valid* one
Time is here

Pencils write what is not to be said
There are some that still care to not tote hearsay around
There are some whom prefer not to look as a clown
Get yours
Own yours
Carry it
Put *theirs* down
12:43 AM 5/16/07

Energy Undefined

I look at you and I see how you are suffering
Never did I force myself on you
With you is where I wanted to be
Yet you didn't fancy me because of your genuine necessity for me

I see the things you are going through and it's killing me to see you hurting
You are down and out

Thoroughly disgusted
Frustrated *internally* I see

You keep your face together
You're well pulled together
People pointed their fingers
I'm standing by you without a doubt
They can't tear me away from you
The only way I'll leave is if you ask me

My professor speaks loudly
At times he is rude
Is it the *chemistry*?
He's not exothermic but endothermic
Ha-ha!

I'm a spring of love
My dynamics cause for you to settle down on your brass ideas
Those once invalid ideals of *yours* no longer make sense to you
I told you but you didn't listen

There is no 'I' in team so why do you think you are all alone?
Every thought that I have is of you
For your safety
You still suffer and I know it
It eats you up inside
Some decisions have been bad ones

I give you my creative energy
I've been here all the time
You opened your hidden garden to me
I saw your secrets
Here they lie…deep inside of me

Today you feel misty blue
Awake my friend
Step up from sleeping
Work
Transfer your energy
Can't you hear the music?
3:22 PM 4/18/07

Dreaming

Guess what?
I have something to say
I believe in you
Wholeheartedly

Today
Forever
You can do anything
You can do more than soar
Pass the farthest stars

If you wish to be a billionaire
That's what you'll be
If you dream of being a rocket scientist
Do it for me

Olympic gold medals
Maybe three
I know *you* can do it
Own two BMW
Seven series

Be United Nations president
You can definitely be
Start a pizza chain
Then take it globally

See your name in lights
On New York, Los Angeles, and Tokyo billboards
Film a movie that you star in
In you I do believe
Reach far
Surpass the farthest star

You've come full circle

Do what I know you do best
Dream aloud then go
Never stop believing
12:36 AM 1/06/07

Hair Stories

Brush my hair
Reddish brown
Wavy and thick

Roots not knits
No knots
No plots

Time passes on
My hair continues to grow
Blow

Blow dry
Not too much heat
Please

Healthy
Long
Strong
Beautiful
Oh, yes

Close cut you have
Pleasing to the touch
Medium fine strands
No gel
Nor grease
That cap
You use please

I glide my hand
Over your bald head

No stubbles in sight
No knick
Nor bruises
It looks shiny

Keep twirling
Your fingers in my hair
It's wavy and fine
Thick at times

Not intertwined
Slick
Deep conditioned
Shampooed
Curled
Never braided
Never locked

"Don't you get a block"
We're *liberated*
Flow down
6:57 PM 12/26/06

Seven In Winter

In the beginning of the winter
Less starry sky
Semi cool air supply
Maximus
Minimus

All
The way
Including us
Demonstrate the new atmosphere
Stepping in
To run out
This is part of the plight

The flight has been cancelled
Until midnight
Heavy breathing
The signs of
Deep love
A few more minutes
Chanting
Sighing
Sign at the 'X'
Not a place of two

We desire truth
Not Bluetooth
Technology is so overbearing

Once you called me *perfection*
Learning the meaning of numbers
I'll be number seven
Lucky seven
Club seven

Unleavened bread
Call me Mia
"Whoa"
Respect me
I *see* you
6:48 PM 12/26/06

Fun And Games

You broke up with me so why are you *hiding* in the bushes?

As I walk to the car I hear the sound of an animal making a loud squealing noise
Oh, *it* is you
What are you doing?
Why are you here?
You have this crazed look upon your face
Gee *weezals*

Is the blue and yellow paint really necessary?
Oh, wow you throw eggs at the car
Do you even realize that it is *your* car?

I was supposed to drop the car back off to you today
After what happened yesterday you should be ashamed
You hit that man in the back of the head
With what?
A bag of old dirty, discolored sweat socks
That old man was my dad's uncle

Yes, I used your car to drop him off
Off at the vet
He believes he has fleas

Oh, crazy you
Oh, crazy me
My car is in the shop for the 18th week
Today is Friday the 13th
Now you want me back

And for sure this time it's a proven fact
I can't get those darn eggs off of your lilac Cadillac
4/26/07

Once Before

Space
The *final* frontier
Where two souls meet
Find their solitude there

People reconcile their differences

Make no excuses

Settle wishes

You will be missed
5:31 PM 4/26/07

300 Plus 1

I long to have an enduring husband such as King Leonidas
He and his 300 men, all Spartans fighting to defend their country to remain forever free
They fought the battle to the very end
For they fought to win
They took no captives
Real men they were
Tried and true
The bravest the world has ever seen or will see

The passion of the queen saved Sparta
She was the strongest woman of her day
Spartans never retreat nor give up
Search your soul, my dear man
Do you have what it takes to be my beloved Spartan man?

To die for their country was to die for their home
Although these 300 plus one men surely did die
They won the war
The Spartan queen sent thousands of men of honor more
When those men died they were free
10:26 PM 5/17/07

Who Are You?

What did you just say?
Why does he continue to cry?

Things are so horrible here
Get out of here

What is going on?
Your words are so strong
Why is he *still* crying?

Maybe today isn't his day
Maybe you say things you ought not to say

I'm just tired of this foolishness
He is crying like a little baby

Hey!
I'm talking to you
I'm a champion
Never call him out of name
Wait your turn for someone to step to you

Your attitude makes you trifling
The stench of your words burn straight through the soul
What goes around comes back around
What day it does?
This no one knows

Watch your mouth
Watch your soul
Do you ever tire yourself out?

Booker T. Washington
Gerald Ford
Everyone knows who they are
No one knows who you are
We wonder why

You cause people's souls to die
11:19 PM 5/15/07

Alone Cries

Said you were coming back but you never did

He was looking for you
Sitting in his lonely window
Rain fell down
Hard drops they fell
Indescribable pain he felt
How could you do it?

30,000 levels up
Down to level 1 up to level 3
Oh, please
5:52 PM 4/26/07

1962

Marilyn Monroe
Who really knows?
How
She died
Was it face up or face down?

Her maid was still in the house

Acts like she didn't hear anything not even a mouse
Marilyn supposedly took dozens of pills so why were none of them found?
Her stomach was empty
Putrefied
That's what they say

They found her body in her own bed but she was most likely killed in the guestroom
In *that* bed
Who moved her body?
Who killed her?
Gees, who knows?

The doctor didn't call the police for maybe another 30 minutes to an hour
Something is wrong
You don't have to be that smart to realize it
Someone had it out for her

It is real sad
Maybe she should have been a nun
Would that make any sense?
That woman was murdered while she was depressed and in distress

Someone knows what happened
But who is that *who*?
I know they were bribed

Kept your silence?
11:32 PM 5/15/07

Sober Thoughts

One *finds* herself through her writings
Just to get it
One
More
Line
A verse
A riddle

A sonnet
Rhymes

She saved lives with those words of hers
Many were forever drowning
Her with her unselfish soul
Kindred heart
Pleasant face
To immensely unfold words of beauty and sanctity

God bless her
Take good care of her
Forgive her of her wrongs
Acknowledge her rights
Not once did she continue to fight

Give her a place of her own
Make her heart happy
Close her eyes
Give her sweet rest

Life continues for her to help someone else
What wonderful place in one's soul
Love's breast
5:44 PM 4/26/07

The Grass Isn't Green

I think of blue grass and sunny skies
Yes, *blue* grass
Small children running free
Old people sitting under maple trees
Under a weeping willow trees is where you'll find me
On a day like today
So sunny and so blue
I love days like this
Oh, yes
2007

Out Of Control

I will rise up out of the ashes
I will live again
The truth to tell you is the beginning *is* the end

Things change
Time goes
I used to believe that I wasn't alive anymore

Circles around
And cats take naps
The weather stays the same
As seasons *are* a changing

Flowers die
Birds sing
Truth in knowing
I'll be here for me

Believe in yourself
The time has come
For you to seek out you
I'll rise again
Yes, I will

Take time for yourself
Find the inner beauty
Who do you want to be?
We only live once
But life continues ongoing

Know me for who I really am
I have not changed
But I *am* changing
Beauty has reflections
Truth knows no bounds

Circles
Many circles circle around
It was brown now it is *light* white
It doesn't look like a night light

Only a few more weeks do we have to spend
You are on your way to *Delusion*, USA
No one helped you prepare for the real world
I *had* once tried
You ignored my suggestions
All the way
What a pity
What a shame
Who is the real person to blame?

I'm so glad I was shown the way
This place is so surreal
Inside your thoughts you are unreal
Believe in yourself, my dear friend
Grow

I'm short
You're tall
Does it make a difference?
No
Not at all
Evolution
Revolution
Disillusion
Confusion
Things all in
One and the same
5:27 PM 4/26/07

Operation Of The Heart, Love And Soul

How can she ever trust him again?
After what he did

It was more than 20 years ago and yet the *memory* still holds on
She was so very young and tenderly sweet
Him with his big feet

Her innocence is long gone
Maybe it is the reason why she never learns how to love
It was not the first time she ran into this particular encounter
Her heart had been shattered
Head wounds she endured
He was supposed to be family
They both were family

Things were said
Things were done
Her soul lies beneath the floor boards
She was very small
Both of her feet could fit into one shoe
A shoe of his

That night she wished she could have run
Silent cries in the night
Would everything be alright?
Now she is seen to be very tense and frightfully uptight
When will she come home?
Maybe not for awhile
Shall she at all?

She is terribly sick
On the contrary, she *will* be fine
She'll go and live with other people
With others she is safe
It's been over 20 years
Perhaps she'll find some rest
Please, open the door
11:48 PM 5/15/07

Gutter Snipe

She's not turning back
Faces in the mirror
Small, quiet and still voices whisper
There's nothing better
She's just in time

The bus draws nearer
She has to escape *this* time
She's been abused and battered for the last time

Torn ligaments
Missing patches of reddish medium length hair
Murdered twin infant sons she can still remember
He killed those boys
Her babies
Their babies
He by no means cared

This woman never called the authorities
She didn't have the strength to tell
Definitely not the strength to leave
An accurate place entitled *Hell*

He was her first love
Known this man since she was thirteen
"Protection order", she says
"What is that?"

She's barely seen on the outside
Her family has no idea
They reside in California

She's been thinking
Contemplating
"How do I get out?"
Echoed sounds of reassurance
"Run!"
"Hurry!"
"Get out!"
She dodged out the back door

Bludgeoned body
Bloody eye
Decayed teeth for lack of nutrition
This man stole her money
How will she survive?

Standing at the bus stop
Dirty bag in hand
A few pieces of bread
And a bottle of honey
She has to get to California

Place of sunshine
No rain

The bus is taking long
Soon he'll be on his way as he is no longer sleeping

As the bus rolls up slowly
He's seen running up
Funny thing is
He's very clumsy
Mr. Lumpy fell
Breaks a leg

The bus door opens
She glides on
Door closes
The man on the ground is so *unfocused*
10:19 PM 5/02/07

Chapter Two: Inspire

The Second Hiatus

Laid Out Flat On The Back

As I sit here
I cry and weep
So many people have been hurt and so many are hurting
The things people go through
Who's willing to reach out their hand?

Gosh, I feel your pain
Allow me the chance to speak
If you need I'll only listen
I'm listening ever so gently

Why do people hurt other's souls?
I wish there would be no child molestation
No ringing gun shots
No slavery
No marital insecurities
No teachers lying
No one has to steal
No one has to drown
Stop committing suicide

There's no need for jealousy or envy
Little girls you do not have to runaway from home
Boys are losing their fathers
People are being stabbed in the back
Small babies are being left in the trunks
Elderly people are pushed away
People in third world countries dying of hunger
People in established countries are dying of hunger *too*
Believe me

Many times we have our backs pushed up against the wall
Fun is made of those who do not dress as everyone else
Animals are brutally tortured by their owners
Yet this is not shown on the Discovery Channel
So many unseen indiscretions and openly done evils
We need help
Lord
8:08 PM 6/17/07

Focus

Must get up on my stuff
Push extra hard
This is not easy but I will make it
I am a *fighter* and I will make it through
There is nothing that I can not do
You may watch me but never aim to stop me

Satan has thrown things out in my path so I will fall
No, so I will fail
I have fallen but I always jump right back up
Irrefutably, he still dwells in *Hell*

So many things in this lifetime to accomplish
I continue to reach up
Yes, you may not know that the sky is the limit

Hey, the sky is not that far so reach for it
You can do it
I know that you can
Life just isn't
That
Bad
2:30 PM 3/19/07

Smiling With Tears

Stop stressing
You are still alive
Life is hard
For this I *do* know
It gets better
Better than this

Stop stressing
My dear
Look up
Keep your focus
The world sometimes looks gray
Tomorrow is a different day
A *new* day

Smile just a little
Don't be so fickle
You are a warrior
Not just a common soldier
You've been made to endure
Hardships won't penetrate your core
Wings on your back to help you soar

Difficulty will arise
Tears in your eyes
Dust settles near you
Rust ruffles you
Get up and
Move
Relocate
Or else *fight*
Fight for your rights
This is *your* life
1:05 AM 12/28/06

On Broken Pieces

Don't you think on your troubles
They'll make you *fly* the coop
Where are your friends?
Where is your family?
Don't they care for you?
Have you pushed them away?
Or have they run away?

Your car needs a jump
Have you changed the oil?
Three of the tires are bare
Where are you going?
There?

Be careful
Watch yourself
No steady work for you
Months and days have passed
Feels as though it's the end
Must make the most
With those *ends*

Continuously run on
Pace yourself
You'll be fine
Cuts on both of your hands
Just make it on broken pieces
If you can

Anything is better than
Not making it at all
Make it if you can
I know you can
And you know you can
1:16 AM 12/2/06

Step Into The New

2007 is only days away
But it is not promised today
Don't quit
Looking at horoscopes
Why?

Meeting up with destiny
You're almost there
Rubbing your hands together
Getting frustrated

You need to know math
5, 6, 7
Yes, lucky 7
7 stand for
Completion
Perfection

Love it
Its coming
This year will be great
Great

Great
Too bad it's not an eight
Strap on your seatbelt
Why worry?
Presenting…the new you

There is time to change
No more resolutions
But make revolutions
Don't slow down
Speed up
It's like making soup
With Swanson's Chicken broth
Deli-cious

Is there a light show?
No
You were wearing braces
Metal
I must see this
It's hilarious

It may be a holiday
Award winning
Driving to town
Today
New Year's Day
Give it harmony

Find something you want
"Hello"
You're going to make it
You're cute
This is important
Harvard
You're on your way
Whistle all the way
Especially, today
1:26 AM 12/28/06

Never Loathe Our Lord

God never lets us down
He's always around
We sometimes wear a frown
But that is not the end
No, it is not my friend

Tidal waves rip and roar
They often times tatter the shore
The children run to their parents
Why does He love us so?
We may never know
We don't deserve Him
He is too good
Simply too good

We always seem to be undone
At times under the gun
He shows up on our behalves
Using blood of clean calves
Once I was mistaken
I thought His love was taken
No place for me
Not at His feet
There's always room for me
It's next to you

Kneeling down in His presence

His love is unmistaken
His love is what we had *taken*
It's so overwhelming
Given to the 6 billion souls
All the ones that fill this earth
You are who He chooses
Reach out your hand
Extend it up
He will overfill your cup

You are His love
Zoom in
8 times optical pixel
Make that 10
Get what He got
A forgiving heart
From you He'll never part
3:19 AM 1/01/07

Wait

I'm sitting here today wondering why things aren't going my way
Well, it is not the way I wish them to go
Doesn't God want us all to excel?
Of course He does

To do better than the day before
Have excellent grades is what I reach for
I mean why not strive to get a 4.00
Do the best that I can
Pre-med

I love being in school
I *love* being in school

College is supposed to be a special chain of events

Succession after succession
Work hard and study hard
Research papers and essays
Writing in calligraphy and Accelerated Trigonometry
These are some of the things that make me think
Think in a good way

Right now I'm struggling so hard to make it
I need all the help I can get
I constantly change my point of view on my life's situation
Searching for the funds
On the lookout for some money, honey

There are times when I'm extremely happy with life and I am super, over-normally positive
Then there are days when I am upset and hurt
Closely nearing a depressed state
When I am down I usually push those close to me away
The shield I put up is a high one to climb over especially on today
And my *unpaid-for-education* is one of the main factors to my upset state
10:13 PM 1/9/07

Inconsistency

Running in place
I am
Trying to escape
The thought of today
Today was rough
But not *so* rough

It was last minute
It was
Hoping to be happy
I'm not going to take my medicine
I don't need it
The pain isn't that bad

I hear the rushing of the river
Otters and bears swim freely
The woods in Glen Ale
That's where you find me
To get away

So tired, gosh!
Close to shutting eyes
Call me later
May be never
Fudgeknuckles!
It's Saturday

I understand
It's time for change
Just let me know
I fell asleep
No one made a scene
Settle down
I'll be upstairs

I fell asleep in that floor's lounge
I hear her coming
"Run!"
Tomorrow will be a better day
You wait and see
The me that you'll see

Slow motion shows inactiveness
It's different now
12:31 AM 12/23/06

Out Of Sight

I'm so excited
I've made it out
Running through *Hell*
Melted my boots
Rain boots

I wasn't well-prepared

Someone stretched out a hand to uplift me
Who could it be?
Whoever it was needs to know
I'm forever grateful
The hand of a king

Calmness passes me
Red hot chili peppers on my sub
Eclipse of the warm sun
Solar beams from above
There are snow caps on the *lunar* moon

I made it out
I choose not to smoke
My lungs would choke
I want to give back
I'll stand by you because you raised me up

Resulting in life you saved me
Somehow
Guess what?
I made it out
It was firestorms in there
My skin almost dried up and blew away
How did I stay so strong?
The real question is: where do I *belong*?

Stitched together I am
Driven through rougher times
Scrubbed down in the mud
Painted on by backstabbers
Life *is* fair, unquestionably so because we can fair weather whatever

Breathtaking mistakes
Monotonous stakes
Go where I want
Ever since
I made it out
9:39 AM 5/02/07

On My Own

I remember the days of loneliness
The feeling of standing alone in a crowd of tens of dozens
Everyone smiling and talking except me
I made *myself* feel this way
I only blame myself

My unfamiliarity to the world
I refuse to be common
Is anything wrong with that?
If I have to stand alone to know who I am
Then so be it
I've been standing on my own for such a long time
But do I have any *qualms*?
4/2007

Class Lecture

The *air* was so thick in there
Thick slices of inconsumable air
The chattering and the bickering was so unnecessary
It all started with the professor

We are here to learn

Who is it that feels as though we lack knowledge?
Aren't we in college?

I am an adult and I have lived a hard life
I came here with the hopes of getting an understanding
Not a *verbal* slapping

Professors and doctors alike have gone to universities
We are here to follow thee
Please do not be sarcastic because I'm an athlete
We are not confused nor are we ignorant
Be pleasant and understanding to me

You changed up in the midst of the storm
Be there for me
I need to know what is going on

We live in this massive etched world
There are so many social barriers that I see
Why can't you take the time out to get to know me?
Know me in my productively

Biased ideals are portrayed daily in these lectures
Smart and irate comments are left in the inbox of students and classmates' minds
This is a place of knowledge
For this is college
A university

Stop staring into space and teach me
My peers have paid *homage* to the thing we call tuition
I'm ready to learn
So teach me

I'm listening and I'm forever willing
We sit on low branches of maples
Looking up to hear what falls from your mouths
I'm listening carefully
Open your mouths

Readily ready for your unspoken words
Reading in between your lines
Ready to learn what happened and what is happening
And you just learned something
You learned it from *us*
12:26 PM 4/27/07

Connective Homes

What a clean house you have
The great upkeep
You've claimed over 300 hundred daisies in your garden
There is a view of the in-ground pool
Bay windows and a scenic view
A white carousel and satin curtains
Cream and brown silk sashes
Pressed linens in the multiple linen closets
Sky blue 450 thread count Egyptian cotton sheet set
Scarlet red duvet spread in California king
Swarovski crystal in almost every visible corner

"Oh there is a picture of Daniel!"
A portrait of Tyra, Eva, Caridee, and Adrienne over the living room sofa for the entire world to see
It's simply beautiful to me
"Please, do not forget Danielle"
Swept and mopped
Clean air filters and hand sanitizers
Carbon monoxide and smoke detectors
Common household unit protectors
China laden with 24 carat gold

Platinum wedding ring sitting in the jewelry box on the dresser
Black tuxedo in his closet
Red cocktail dress in her closet
Football trophy on display
Manolo Blahnik, Stacy Adams, and Jimmy Choo shoes galore
Bose surround sound system in the personal home theater
1100 gallon aquarium with approximately 400 different fish swimming through it
The way a gorgeous home should be
1:24 AM 1/06/07

To See You

I wish it was Mother's Day
Yet, every day is
You were my best friend
Still is

It's been some years since you went away
You told me about life
All things moral
All things true
Thick skinned you were
Shallow I was
So shallow that I still hurt

I need a little luck
Wishing to see you again
You once said that love was a misunderstanding between two fools
Well, I'm the greatest fool
A fool I choose

Red face, black cap, yellow nose, orange toes
I'll stand by you and I won't let anybody hurt you
Even though you're gone
9:45 PM 5/02/2007

Ballet Insight

Powdery pink ballerina skirts twirl
The sight of flat toed slippers whisk smooth across the hard wood stage
Silent sounds of beauty perfect the scene
Light green silk draperies align the front drop of the dimly lit theater
As guests enter the foyer sweet aromas fill the air
What a wonderful sight to behold

Pictures of the greatest ballets of all time hang along the lilac and golden walls
Young adolescent girls dream of one day becoming ballerinas in these beautiful theatres
Dreams come true
And some dreams crossover

Little girls, hold on to your dreams
Powdery pink ballerina skirts twirl
Adoring fairies everyway
If this is what you want to be; you can be
Be who *you* want to be
7:18 PM 5/17/07

The Children

I look out the window and all I see is blood in the streets
Where is it coming from?
Who is doing this?
What is happening?
And where are the children?

This makes no sense to me
Why is everyone killing one another?
Why do they act so?
There used to be a place to go to get away from everything
Remember when we were able to walk through the park?
Play marbles and hop-scotch?
And eat on the open porch when it was dark?
The cares of the every day rustic as we call them affects us, one in all

Stop hurting the children
The children are crying aloud for us to help them
Stand up and fight for them
They are our future
They are all we have
The world needs them
We need them
Their futures could be oh so bright
Yet this world is trying its best to destroy their hope, to steal their light

Love comes not without a price
Nonetheless, the price is not high
Love each child as if he were your own
Do what you must for them
Make this the best place for them to be
Everyone only gets one chance to make it in this life
Allow these little ones to have the chance that we never had
Ones to come after us should be taught by us
For we know the way
We were taught from those of the past

Lives *unlived* yesterday
Look into the children's eyes
They are waiting and longing to be loved
We have the responsibility of teaching them
They have the right to be taught
Get it together
Show them the way
Today is surely their day
Tomorrow is no longer *ours*
3:13 PM 3/24/2007

Children Of War

There is no greater love than that of a parent for his child
A parent would lay down his life for a child
Children have need of their parents
Parents are their lifeline

Their source of survival

In the news we see parents being murdered before their children's eyes
And children being raped and slaughtered before their parents
How can someone hurt a child?
Where does this hatred come from?
Let love abound
Allow peace to flow through our *harts*

Unused love melts into hate
Allow love to be oxygen in your life
A much needed resource
There is a degree of resistance to hate-ability
That degree of measurement is *understanding*
We must take time to understand one another
We irresistibly must have the priority of communication
Lack of communication seems to be the number one cause of our eternal problems

No one anymore wishes to let their light shine through
Why do we all wish to be clones?
God made us all to be leaders
Lead by example, yet pay close attention to others' mistakes and misfortunes

Please excuse my boldness
Is President Bush a terrorist?
He murders many through this conspiracy named the Iraq War
Iraqis and Americans are dying daily
Families wait to see their loved ones return home but again they have been called away
There are some parents who have given up their lives for their children
If you die don't die in vain
Don't leave your page an empty page
Bush has less than 690 days left to cause our *only* two allies to go insane
3:09 PM 4/18/07

A Way With Words

Whispering wondrous words of wisdom
Laying lovely beneath light leaves on limbs

Never underestimate new numbers before nuisance
Defy all definitive deaths of demo displays
Explain explosive expressions of excruciating exposures

Hats on hollowly hilled halls of heated heights
Magical music memories over mortified mothers making more
Always achieving abandonment above actual aggravated attachment
Consider closing colorful caskets during confused comments

Sappy soliloquies staged by smells of solid solitudes of seven savages
Beautiful belittled bountiful blessings beneath and before beached bays of blue boots
Open all obsessions on oppressive outwards
2:43 PM 5/21/07

Breakfast At Tiffany's

She continues to cry
Didn't get what she wanted
Being stubborn
Making things hard
For only herself

Mother, father, sister
Attempt to please her
Had an overwhelming Christmas
Running because Jeopardy is now on
At times
Well, all the time
Is it true?
Yes, it's true

She runs and runs
And screams
She is only three
Can you believe that she?
Screams and screams
Runs so free
Hits even me

112

Laugh
Always
Always
I mean always
Laughing
She is hilarious
She's a baby
I hear her mother
Say "stop it"
Twice
I wonder why

She's her *own* person
Grown already
She must have been here before
When she's bad
She's bad
But she's a baby
Wrist way smaller than yours and mine
Repeatedly calling out "mommy"
Does she hear her?
Babies never give up
Staying on the move

Watching Barney and Dora
Knowing her ABC's
When she feels the mood
Counting her numbers to skip number six
And she knows
Tell her and she
Laughs
Is that bad?
She's a baby

Running fast
Putting on her sister's skate
They are almost a size eight
She is very little
Weighing in at
Under 42 pounds
Got to get her in the kitchen
Eat her favorite snack
String beans
Cucumbers with some ranch
7:31 PM 12/26/06

When I Grow Up

Feel the sunlight on your face
Little child
Hear what I say
Today is a better day
Don't let what they say
Push you away

You are great
You were made
By God, not man
He is the Great One
The Only One

All things are *possible*
To them that believe
Take up your bed
Go, ahead
Walk
Run
Dream

Dream of things to come
Lovely and new

This is the earth
It belongs to you
Paint the sky *bleu*
Oh, it is blue

Charge up the battery
It needs to be used
Don't let it die
Go, ahead
Fly

Buy a kite
Better yet make your own
This time is yours

Put on your clothes
The ones you own
Not that red, blue, and green stuff
The *colors* you painted
The walls in that shop were already tainted
Life is what you make it
3:06 AM 1/01/07

Knights Of The Roundtable

Simply beautiful this is
Today is a gorgeous day
Just took a fabulous bubble filled bath in Sugared Lemongrass

As I glance out the bay window
I'm figuring out what to wear
I have to go and make this a special day

Oh, man, my birthday is near
I'm not even happy because of that
Well, maybe I am for it will be another year

Year in this life of mine
I'm happy because I'm getting together with my buddies
My comrades

Gosh, I'm pretty
Pretty happy to be
Loved and cherished by *thee*

Oh! I know what I'll wear
My red sundress with the pink stripes
I must have the perfect accessories

Pull my hair up with seven pieces of golden ribbon

Oh, this is so very cute
Take my picture would you?

I want to remember this
Wait!
I almost forgot my oversized Gucci sunglasses

Call my friends up so we can have a night on the town
Tonight I'm not driving
I want to be chauffeured around

I am not at all persnickety
I am just over zealously happy to be
To be free
In the company of my cherished friends
Is where I choose to be

No worries, I tell thee
I know what I want and I must go after it
This world is full of life
Just look around

I do not wish to look like a bag of Skittles for I am over the age of 21
Certain looks are only for kids and I mean small kids
I love to wear various colors but not *all* at the same time

Oops!
Back to what I was saying
Call my friends
They are all marvelously sexy
My male and female friends alike

Remind them that the day must begin with some shopping
Yes, it's my treat
My only request is that you be on time
Promptness is surely not a crime
Those who are late don't get asked out a second time

Right about now I could go for some Red Lobster
I hope they're not crowded
Maybe, it's lunchtime
Hopefully, we'll be able to get a roundtable
Do you enjoy Maine lobster?

I'm glad I got my French Manicure on yesterday
Must keep one's self looking right
Skin so sweetly kissed by my favorite perfume Magnetic Beat

Today is a day for friends
To be justly in high spirits
Smooches!
I love you guys

You guys look so wonderful
The light hits your face just right

When you receive a first edition you receive the first copy and let alone the best copy
Friends are the first editions of our lives
Come on, guys
We're going to a salsa club to do a little dance
How about the Mambo?
Man, you got to love these stilettos

It's not a bad day
The air is just right
Gosh, it's perfect
All of my friends are here
We're gathered around

Never have we been cultish nor pushed others around
We don't gossip about others; that's not how we get down
We are not mean and we don't need to take over any town

We are ladies and gents; our parents raised us right
We travel, educate, reciprocate to the community and ultimately are merry
Some are from the country, several from the suburbs, and others the city

It doesn't make a difference any of our backgrounds
Just the contentment each of us gets when one flashes an immediate smile
Zippy zip
Could I be any happier?
Not!
Those are my knights
Knights of the great *round*
My friends I'm talking about
10:10 PM 6/17/07

Don't Stop Believing

I wish that you would move
I wish that you would get up

Let your fears drown
Liven up your spirits
Fly high

It's as being in love for the first time
You have the *ability* to recharge
You have tons of new ideas
We are here to help you rebuild
The sky couldn't be any bluer
The destination couldn't be any closer
Accelerate

You tried to jump over the edge
But God built you a hedge
You thought you were cursed
You've been blessed by the best
It is time for you to listen
You must believe
From the inside out
Through and through

You took a sneak peak into your future
Almost everyone knew
You had become afraid
What you had saw startled you
It was so overwhelming and very powerful
You were truthfully elated
You believed you'd make it
Once upon you did

Nations have changed
People did not remain the same
Some attempted to show your shame

Who caused you to stop believing?
Who stole your English muffin?
I'm counting on you
When you hear from your heart
You feel at home

We are here to give you ultimate protection
We wish to make your life colorful
Yet you have to be the one to dream

While others fade away you must stay the same
Brilliant and bright
You are extremely bright
You do not need psychiatric care

You are no longer a victim of violence
No one can steal your trophy
Let the record show

Reflections of what you used to be
I report accuracy and consistency
It's been proven to be
This report in my hands state that you are destined to make it

Believe
In yourself
This is no longer a dream
This is reality
Can you see?
You must close your eyes at times to see what must be seen
Seek to follow the non-stop light
What you believe you saw is *right*
2:22 AM 7/17/07

Concluding Remarks

I am quite elated that you have taken some time out of your schedule to read my book *Not Today*. While ideas that I have shared with you are far from being perfect and faultless, they are my surveillances on subjects of love, trust, friendship, and optimism. Nothing that have I stated has been intended to neither offend anyone nor damage their character. What I have stated is only projected to give you something to think on. My expressions are to ultimately allow you a much needed cry or a good laugh.

On the Day He Died and *Nor Tomorrow* will be on the available within the next two years. *On the Day He Died* is a so-close-to-real fictional story with first and secondhand narration of an abused man. *Nor Tomorrow* is another collection of poems, short stories and axioms that will make you laugh hysterically and others will force you to think on a few indisputable lifetime changes we often incur.

My wish is that we help one another however we can. We may perhaps start a chain reaction if we would simply offer a kind word or an effortless smile. There is way too much violence and hatred in this world. Jealousy and strife has taken over once stable friendships and acquaintances. We must attempt to recognize but reverence our differences and discuss our vast similarities. We are all different and yet we are all the same but there is no need to be indifferent. Be who you were born to be. Be you.

Do not worry about a thing. Worrying does not make it any better. God is in control of everything. I do not know when things will look up or how but they will. Know in the end that everything will be alright. Never stop believing.

"And now abideth faith, hope, charity, these three; but the greatest of these is charity."

-I Corinthians 13:13

Love is exceedingly and thoroughly contagious; infect someone.

With love,

Minimah Billings
A.k.a.
3 Free Falling

Under a weeping willow tree is where you'll find me…

www.ingramcontent.com/pod-product-compliance
Lightning Source LLC
Chambersburg PA
CBHW080914020726
47502CB00008B/2451